Venus

Earth

Asteroid Belt

Saturn

Neptune

Project
Mercury

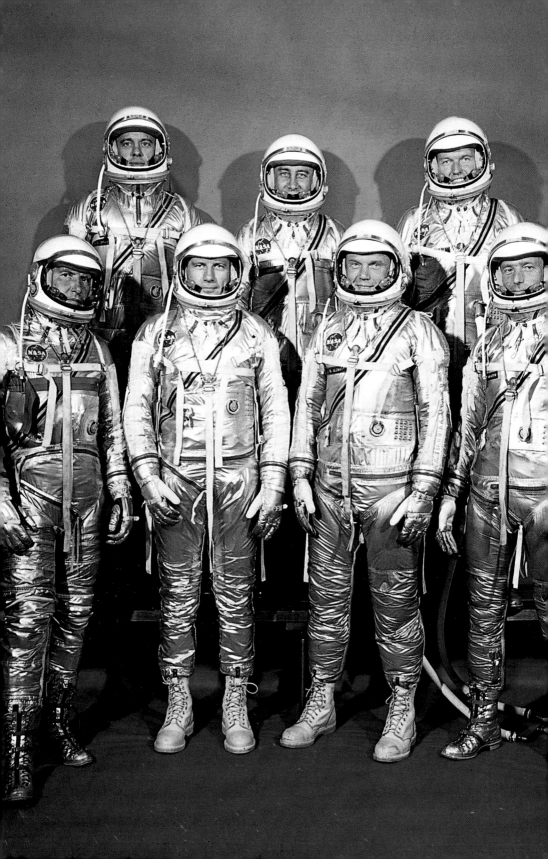

Project
Mercury

Ray Spangenburg and Kit Moser

Franklin Watts

A DIVISION OF GROLIER PUBLISHING
NEW YORK · LONDON · HONG KONG · SYDNEY
DANBURY, CONNECTICUT

In memory of
ROBERT GODDARD,
rocket scientist, engineer,
and visionary

Photographs ©: Corbis-Bettmann: 63 (Reuters New Media Inc.), 20, 22, 24, 30, 45 (UPI), 58; NASA: cover, 2, 8, 10, 12, 14, 29, 33, 35, 39, 41, 47, 51, 55, 56, 59, 61, 67, 69, 71, 74, 76, 79, 81, 83, 84, 87, 89, 90, 100, 103, 104; National Air and Space Museum, Smithsonian Institution: 26, 37; Photri-Microstock: 19; Sovfoto/Eastfoto: 18, 43, 66, 96.

The photograph on the cover shows *Mercury-Atlas 6* lifting off on February 20, 1962. The photograph opposite the title page shows the Mercury Seven astronauts.

Visit Franklin Watts on the Internet at:
http://publishing.grolier.com

Library of Congress Cataloging-in-Publication Data

Spangenburg, Ray.
        Project Mercury / by Ray Spangenburg and Kit Moser.
            p.   cm.—(Out of this world)
        Includes bibliographical references and index.
        Summary: Describes the planning, development, missions, and accomplishments of Project Mercury and its contributions to the American presence in space.
        ISBN 0-531-11763-4 (lib. bdg.)   0-531-13974-3 (pbk.)
        1. Project Mercury (U.S.)—History—Juvenile literature. [1. Project Mercury (U.S.) 2. Space—Exploration.] I. Moser, Diane, 1944- II. Title. III. Out of this world (Franklin Watts, Inc.)

TL789.8.U6 M4837   2001
629.45'4'0973—dc21   00-027010

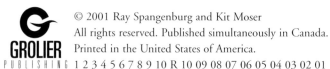
© 2001 Ray Spangenburg and Kit Moser
All rights reserved. Published simultaneously in Canada.
Printed in the United States of America.
1 2 3 4 5 6 7 8 9 10 R 10 09 08 07 06 05 04 03 02 01

Acknowledgments

We would like to thank the many people who have contributed to *Project Mercury*. First of all, special appreciation goes to Melissa Stewart, our editor at Franklin Watts, whose steady flow of creativity, energy, enthusiasm, and dedication have infused this series. Our thanks also to NASA Chief Historian Roger D. Launius and Sam Storch, lecturer at the American Museum-Hayden Planetarium, who both made many helpful suggestions. To Tony Reichhardt and John Rhea, once our editors at the former *Space World Magazine,* thanks for starting us out on the fascinating journey we have taken during our years of writing about space.

Contents

Liftoff! *Freedom 7* and Alan Shepard take off for space.

May 5, 1961

Alan Shepard felt as if he weighed about 1,000 pounds (450 kilograms) as he blasted into space. His body labored to function normally under six times the force of normal Earth gravity. The instrument panel in Shepard's tiny spacecraft rocked and rolled wildly before him as he blinked, trying to regain his composure.

Years of preparation had gone into this moment. Shepard was about to become the first American to enter space.

Shepard's day had begun well before dawn. He had eaten what is now considered the traditional astronaut's launch-morning breakfast of steak and eggs. By 5:15 A.M., he had arrived at the launchpad. There, the Redstone rocket stood ready, with the tiny *Freedom 7* cap-

Just moments before liftoff, NASA technicians check on Alan Shepard.

sule perched at the top. Soon, Shepard was strapped into the cramped cabin of the space capsule.

Finally, after more than four tedious, worrisome hours of waiting atop the rocket—Liftoff! The mighty Redstone rocket thundered and rose into the air, boosting the small capsule and its lone pilot skyward.

Now it was time for the Mercury capsule to separate from the Redstone *booster* rocket. Then *Freedom 7* would soar alone in a wide arc that would make space history.

"All systems go," Shepard reported calmly to Mission Control.

Quickly and systematically, the link between the capsule and the booster rocket was broken. The Redstone engine shut down and the separation rockets at the base of *Freedom 7* fired to push the capsule away from the spent booster rocket.

Suddenly, everything changed. Moments before, Shepard's environment had seemed violent and noisy. His body had fought against incredible pressures. Now everything seemed incredibly peaceful. Shepard was weightless inside the capsule's cramped cabin.

Freedom 7 was moving on its own, leaving the big booster behind. It was May 5, 1961. America's first astronaut had arrived in space.

A Space Shuttle crew heads for another work day in space.

Chapter 1

The Space Age Begins

At one time, adventures in space existed only in science-fiction stories and the dreams of a few bold scientists and engineers. Today space flights are an everyday reality. By the end of the twentieth century, many American astronauts had spent more than ten consecutive days in space. Shuttle missions occurred without mishap several times a year. They had become so routine that they rarely even made the television news. Yet, even today, the adventures of working, living, and traveling in space remain very new.

The story of humans in space begins with *Sputnik 1*, the first "space traveler" ever launched by humans. *Sputnik 1* was only about 24 inches (61 centimeters) across and weighed a mere 184 pounds (83 kg), but it proved an important point: Humans could build a space-craft and launch it into *orbit* around Earth.

Sputnik 1 was an enormously important scientific first. It was also the first chess move in a political contest that began one of the most bold and daring adventures ever undertaken—human exploration of space.

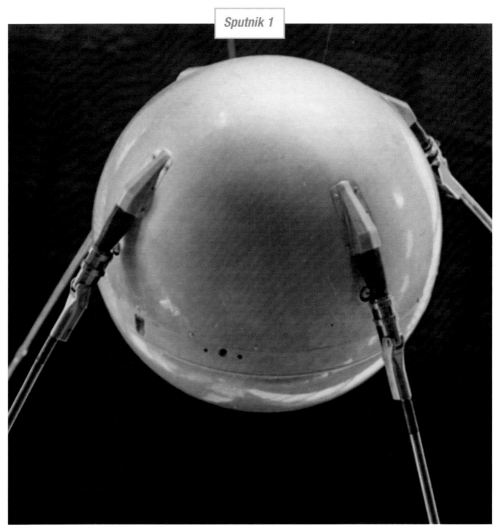

Sputnik 1

Stranger in the Sky

On October 4, 1957, Americans looked up at the nighttime sky to catch a glimpse of *Sputnik 1* orbiting Earth. What they saw amazed and horrified them. As they watched the spacecraft whiz across the sky—its shiny exterior reflecting the light of the Sun—they knew they stood at the brink of an exciting new era. Yet, *Sputnik's* blinking light also filled them with dread. This extraordinary spacecraft had been launched by the Soviet Union, a nation that was unfriendly to the United States.

People in many parts of the world viewed *Sputnik 1* with great reserve. The Soviet Union, also known as the Union of Soviet Socialist Republics (USSR), had formed following the Russian Revolution of 1917. It united Russia, Ukraine, Belarus, and several other countries in Central Asia, Eastern Europe, and the Balkan Peninsula. The Communist government that had come to power in the new union—dominated by the Russian Communist Party—had quickly developed into a powerful, tyrannical dictatorship. For 74 years, the Soviet Union was

How Science Works: Putting an Object in Orbit

Imagine climbing to the top of a tall mountain and throwing a ball as hard as you can. The harder you throw the ball, the farther it will go before Earth's gravity wins out and pulls it to the ground. If you were exceptionally strong—say, as powerful as the rocket used to launch *Sputnik 1*—you could make the ball travel faster than 17,500 miles (28,163 kilometers) per hour. At this speed, the ball would arc up across the sky and whiz into space. Earth's gravity would prevent the ball from soaring on to the Moon or beyond, but gravity's pull would not win out completely. The ball would not fall back to the ground. Instead, the ball's acceleration would keep it going, and Earth's gravity would keep the ball in orbit. The ball would revolve around Earth, in much the same way that *Sputnik 1* orbited Earth.

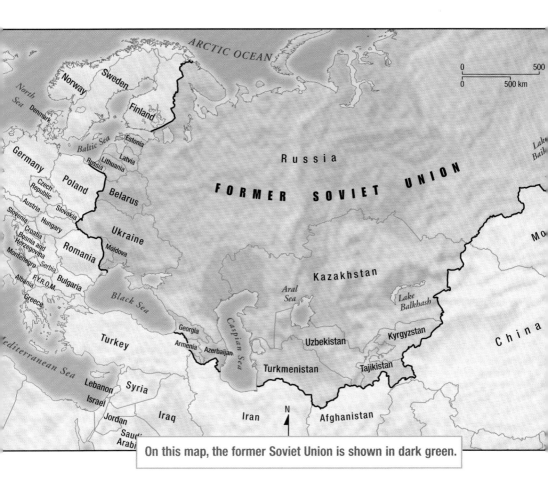

On this map, the former Soviet Union is shown in dark green.

one of the strongest political and military forces in the world.* During that time, most non-Communist countries viewed Soviet power as an enormous threat to freedom and democracy.

In the years following World War II (1939-1945), the United States and the Soviet Union became increasingly hostile, even though they were not technically at war. By 1957, they had entered a period

* The Soviet Union disintegrated in 1991.

known as the "Cold War." Each country believed that a "hot," fighting war might break out at any time, and they stockpiled nuclear weapons and competed fiercely for worldwide influence and esteem.

During this period, the U.S. and Soviet governments competed to show superiority. Each nation believed that establishing a presence in space could display its competence in science and engineering.

The year 1957 was the International Geophysical Year. Nations worldwide were working on projects to further scientific exploration of our home planet. Launching a spacecraft would fit nicely with the goals set for the International Geophysical Year and, at the same time, imply military strength. After all, rockets that could soar into space could also be aimed, with a warhead attached, at any country in the world. No one was likely to miss this political message.

Both the United States and the Soviet Union believed that having superior rockets and space technology would demonstrate their power and prestige. A "space race" began, kicked off by the launch of *Sputnik 1*. No one had any question about who had won the first leg of the race.

So, even though the United States did not put *Sputnik 1* into orbit, this historic feat was the first step toward the American presence in space. It also proved to be the first step in America's voyage to the Moon.

Trying to Catch Up

On November 3, 1957, about a month after the launch of *Sputnik 1*, the Soviets lobbed an even larger satellite into space. *Sputnik 2* weighed 1,140 pounds (517 kg). Putting an object like that into orbit demonstrated tremendous rocket power and technological expertise. *Sputnik 2* also carried a small dog named Laika into the weightlessness

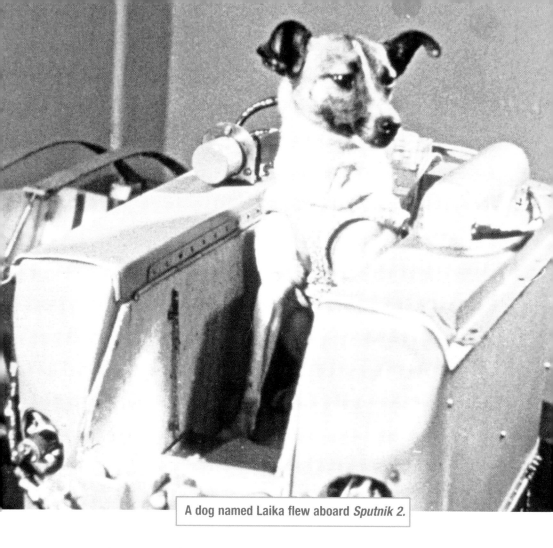

A dog named Laika flew aboard *Sputnik 2.*

and vacuum of space.* *Sputnik 2* showed the world that the Soviets had serious plans for space.

The two Sputnik spacecraft were an intense embarrassment to the United States. In the world's eyes, Soviet technology and might were superior. If Americans wanted to win back the respect they had enjoyed since World War II, they would have to prove that they were equal to the Soviet Union.

* Former Soviet space administrators have since expressed regret about sending Laika into space without knowing how to get her back.

The good news was that an existing U.S. Army missile named Jupiter-C was capable of launching a satellite. The bad news was that the U.S. government preferred not to put this particular rocket in the spotlight. The team of engineers that had built it was the same group who had designed and built the V-2 rocket for Nazi Germany. During World War II, the Nazis had used the V-2 to bomb U.S. allies.

This German V-2 rocket was brought to the United States for testing.

At the end of the war, the U.S. government invited the German rocket engineers to come to the United States.* By 1957, the German engineers had become U.S. citizens. Led by Wernher von Braun, they were working for the U.S. Army in New Mexico and Alabama. Thanks to their help, the U.S. Army was ready with a rocket powerful enough to launch a satellite, and the group probably could have achieved this important goal before the Soviets launched *Sputnik 1.*

U.S. President Dwight D. Eisenhower knew that the German rocket team was ready to go, but he faced a dilemma. He was convinced that launching a scientific satellite with an Army rocket would make a bad impression on the rest of the world. Eisenhower was also aware of the diplomatic delicacy of using a rocket based on the design of the V-2 and built by the very men whose rockets had bombed U.S. allies during World War II.

To avoid a public-relations blunder, Eisenhower asked the Naval Research Laboratory to speed up the development of

President Dwight D. Eisenhower

---

* The Soviet government had also invited some of the German rocket team to their country after the war. Like the United States, the Soviet Union knew the value of these men. Because the Soviets kept a great deal of information secret, few people knew that some German scientists were hard at work in the Soviet Union.

its Viking rocket. Although the Viking needed a little more work, the U.S. government pushed ahead. In the minds of Americans and their allies, the space race was a battle between the power of freedom, democracy, and capitalism versus the prowess of a communist dictatorship. It was very important that the Viking rocket succeed in putting a U.S. satellite into orbit, and that the launch happen as soon as possible.

On December 6, 1957, just a month after the second *Sputnik* launch, the Viking rocket stood on the launchpad, ready for countdown. Its "passenger" was *Vanguard*, a tiny, 6-inch (15-cm) sphere that the tall, slender rocket would speed skyward into Earth orbit. People all over the United States held their breath as the countdown ended. The Viking roared, rose a few inches and, in one disastrous moment,

How a Rocket Works

Have you ever blown up a balloon and then let go of it? As you add air to a balloon, the pressure inside builds up. Air presses against the walls of the balloon equally in every direction. When you let go of the balloon, air rushes out in one direction. This causes an imbalance inside the balloon. The air inside the balloon presses hardest against the forward wall, propelling it in the direction opposite the escaping gas.

According to Isaac Newton's third law of motion, for every action there is an equal and opposite reaction. In other words, when something is pushed forward, something else must move backward the same amount. An inflated balloon expelling air obeys this law. So does a rocket releasing a steady stream of exhaust.

The gas molecules that make up rocket exhaust are produced as fuel burns inside a rocket's engine. The forces of action and reaction, which propel the rocket forward, occur the moment the fuel is burned—before exhaust leaves the engine.

The movement of a rocket does not depend on anything outside the engine. A rocket is not propelled forward because its exhaust pushes against air. This is an important idea because space is a vacuum—it contains no air. In space, there is absolutely nothing to push against.

As NASA technicians made a final check of *Vanguard* and its Viking rocket, no one imagined that the satellite would never make it to space.

collapsed to the ground. The little *Vanguard* satellite bounced from the top of the rocket and rolled away into the shrubs, where it began forlornly beeping. This was not the beginning the United States had hoped for.

Rocket to the Rescue

Now Eisenhower had no choice. He knew the United States had to launch a *satellite* as soon as possible, so he asked von Braun and his team for help. These men had been working together on rockets for years. Some of them had started out with von Braun as teenage members of a rocket club in Germany. Most of them had always hoped to launch rockets that could take humans into space. Now their experience and readiness paid off. They quickly modified the Army's four-stage Jupiter-C rocket. It also received a new, gentler name—Juno 1 (in honor of Jupiter's wife in Roman mythology).

Meanwhile, another team of engineers at the Jet Propulsion Laboratory (JPL) in Pasadena, California, built a satellite called *Explorer 1*. At just 6.7 feet (2 m) long and 6.5 inches (16.5 cm) in diameter, it was larger than the *Vanguard* satellite but still much smaller than the Sputnik satellites. The engineers outfitted *Vanguard* with a series of scientific experiments designed by James Van Allen, a professor at the University of Iowa.

Finally, everything was ready and the day for launch— January 31, 1958—arrived. This time, the rocket worked. *Explorer 1* soared into space, and on its way, it discovered one of the Van Allen radiation belts, a region of radiation between 620 and 3,000 miles (998 and 4,828 km) above Earth's equator. The United States had arrived in space at last.

NASA Is Born

The road to success in space was not smooth though. The next attempt to launch using the Navy's Viking rocket failed. *Explorer 2,* aboard another Juno rocket, also fizzled. The first successful *Vanguard* finally

A modified Army Jupiter-C rocket carries the first U.S. satellite, *Explorer 1*, into space.

soared into space in March 1958. Meanwhile, the Soviet Union launched *Sputnik 3* in May. At 2,978 pounds (1,351 kg), it was even bigger and more impressive than the first two Sputniks.

By now, space was in the news all over the world. If the United States wanted to compete with the Soviet Union in this arena, bold steps would be needed. To pave the way, on July 29, President Eisenhower signed the National Aeronautics and Space Act of 1958. With that act, the National Aeronautics and Space Administration (NASA) was born. The new agency opened for business on October 1.

Less than 3 months later, on December 17, NASA made a stunning announcement: A new program would send pilots into space. NASA called the program Project Mercury, after the messenger of the gods in Roman mythology.

The X-1 is now on display at the Smithsonian's Air and Space Museum in Washington, D.C.

Chapter 2

The Mercury Seven

Many big challenges lay ahead. The scientists and engineers at NASA had to come up with an effective, safe plan for getting astronauts into space. Would they fly into space on a winged rocket plane—something like the X-1 experimental plane that Chuck Yeager had used to break the sound barrier in 1947? If so, it would have to be faster, more powerful, and able to fly in the vacuum of space. Perhaps it would be better for astronauts to ride into space in a satellitelike capsule atop a rocket.

Once the astronauts left Earth's atmosphere, how would they survive in the harshness of space—a place that is extremely cold and has no oxygen, no air pressure, and no gravity? Could human beings adjust to the weightlessness they would experience in space? Could they think clearly and work effectively? And finally, how would these astronauts return to Earth?

The goals of Project Mercury were to place a piloted spacecraft in orbit and to demonstrate the ability of humans to survive and work well in space.

Choosing Astronauts

Perhaps the most important question was who would make these first journeys into space? The people chosen would have the honor of being among the first to venture into this new frontier. The challenges would be both exciting and enormously dangerous.

By February 1959, the selection process for astronauts was well under way. NASA looked first at military test pilots. These fliers already understood the risks of piloting experimental craft. They had proven courage and steady nerves. They were already used to the dangers of reduced air pressure and the need for special protective gear. They had also shown that they could function extremely well under stress. And they had proved they had no hint of claustrophobia—an important trait, since they would be traveling in a spacecraft about the size of a telephone booth. The spacecraft would be so small, in fact, that the first astronauts could be no taller than 5 feet 11 inches (180 cm).

Thousands of people showed interest in the job, and from these NASA selected 110 military test pilots. In April 1959, seven of the finalists became the first astronauts. Their names soon became famous: M. Scott Carpenter, L. Gordon Cooper Jr., John H. Glenn Jr., Virgil I. "Gus" Grissom, Walter M. "Wally" Schirra Jr., Alan B. Shepard Jr., and Donald K. "Deke" Slayton. Three were Navy test pilots, three were Air Force test pilots, and one, John Glenn, was a Marine Corps pilot.

The Mercury Seven, the first U.S. astronauts

These seven were all experienced pilots in their 30s. They were all the first born in their families—a trait psychologists say contributed to their high achievement goals and willingness to take risks. They all came from small towns and middle-class families. Most had studied at military academies or state universities. Many had been Boy Scouts as kids and had earned numerous badges and high rank. They were all intelligent and quick to learn. They all loved to race, take risks, fly hard and high, and overcome tough challenges. They seemed to be exactly what NASA had in mind—representatives of American democracy.

Jerrie Cobb and the "Mercury Thirteen"

Few people know that a group of women also hoped to be selected as astronauts. Among them was Jerrie Cobb, who learned to fly an airplane when she was 12 and first flew solo at 16. During her teen years, Cobb played semiprofessional women's softball for the Oklahoma City Queens so that she could earn enough money to buy her first airplane. By the age of 21, she was a certified flight instructor. From then on, there was no stopping her.

She flew dangerous missions over jungles, and she patrolled pipelines. She broke international speed and distance records. She flew crop dusters, gliders, blimps, and B-17 four-engine bombers. Cobb loved flying and hoped to be the first woman in space. For a very brief time in 1960, it almost looked as if her dream would come true.

A few months after the original Mercury Seven astronauts were selected, Jerrie Cobb and twelve other top women pilots were selected for a private program that would put them through the same rigorous testing procedures as the Mercury Seven astronauts. The thirteen women, including Jerrie, passed the demanding tests with flying colors.

However, NASA ruled that American astronauts also had to be qualified jet test pilots, and in those days, only men were allowed to train as military jet pilots. Jerrie and the other "Mercury Thirteen" protested. They even took their case to Congress, but the hearings lost momentum after astronaut John Glenn gave his testimony. He supported the position, popular at the time, that such jobs were best left up to men.

Disappointed, Jerrie quit her job as an executive for an Oklahoma City airplane manufacturer and became a flying missionary, carrying supplies, food, and medicine deep into the dangerous jungles of Central and South America. She remains there today, still flying missions and working with native tribes.

In 1995, when Eileen Collins was chosen as the pilot for a Space Shuttle *Discovery* mission, Collins invited Jerrie Cobb to attend the launch. It was the first U.S. spaceflight piloted by a woman. By the end of the 1990s, 25 women in the U.S. space program had set records of 10 days or more in space.

Jerrie Cobb

Getting Ready for Space

At a news conference shortly after the seven Mercury astronauts were selected, one reporter asked the most dramatic question of the day, "Can I have a show of hands on how many of you are confident that they will come back from outer space?" Without hesitation, all seven raised their hands. In fact, John Glenn raised both hands.

Courage and confidence unquestionably were part of the "right stuff" required of these men, as portrayed in Tom Wolfe's book of that name (and the movie based on it). The astronauts' training was also strenuous—both intellectually and physically. They attended lectures about astronautics. They learned about the spacecraft, rockets, spacesuits, and other equipment they would be using. They tried out the spacesuits in varying environments, including low-pressure chambers, a *centrifuge*, and weightless flying.

From inside a centrifuge—a machine that spins to simulate the increased gravity of liftoff, reentry, and braking—the astronauts tested their ability to maintain the capsule *attitude* and speed and to deal with various potential emergencies. They also rode as passengers aboard planes that made steep climbs followed by sudden drops to create *zero gravity*, or weightlessness, for a few seconds at a time.

They used procedures trainers—mechanical simulators of the Mercury spacecraft they would fly—to test the spacecraft's controls and get a sense of what it would be like to operate them. Using the centrifuge and the procedures trainers, the astronauts were able to experience most of the situations they would face during flight. Another special trainer showed the astronauts what they might expect to see through the capsule periscope or window, including a simulation of Earth's horizon. They could use this trainer to practice con-

Astronaut training was strenuous, technical, and dangerous. However, the astronauts were amused to find themselves also being coached on how to look suave and heroic in public. They were told to wear long knee socks, so that unattractive lengths of bare leg wouldn't show when they crossed their legs on a stage. Their appearance training even touched on the "more masculine" way to stand with hands on hips. Apparently, thumbs back, fingers forward was the preferred position. Most took this advice with good humor and concentrated on the training that would help them stay alive in the harsh environment of space.

trolling the spacecraft's attitude during orbit and reentry. An additional device helped the astronauts train for the physical and psychological effects that would occur if their spacecraft began tumbling. It also gave them practice in bringing the spacecraft back under control.

At the Morehead Planetarium in Chapel Hill, North Carolina, the astronauts studied how to navigate by the stars and learned to recognize key stars. They completed a $5\frac{1}{2}$-day course in desert survival at the U.S. Air Force Training Command Survival School.

The Mercury missions would all land at sea, in a maneuver known as a "splashdown." After an astronaut's capsule splashed into the water, it was up to him to get out of the spacecraft so that a helicopter rescue team could pick him up. In training, each astronaut made at least two exits from the upper hatch, sometimes in fairly heavy seas. The astronauts also trained for a side-hatch exit and practiced getting out of the spacecraft underwater.

Meanwhile, all the astronauts continued to fly airplanes as part of their training, and since they all loved flying nearly as much as breathing, they often spent weekends flying together across the country.

The Mercury Seven were all test pilots, here suited up for flight: (left to right) Carpenter, Cooper, Glenn, Grissom, Schirra, Shepard, and Slayton.

Chapter 3

Travel Plans

Meanwhile, as the astronauts prepared for the rigors of space, engineers and scientists were working on transportation—the first stagecoach to space and the horsepower to take it there. The fliers of the X-series of experimental planes had flown high—into the near-space regions of the atmosphere. Most of the pilots, and many of the engineers who built and maintained the aircraft, thought a "space plane" might work. However, worries about the heat of reentry presented too many challenges for a winged spacecraft. When an object enters Earth's atmosphere, friction causes intense heat. So, the Mercury spacecraft would be a specially designed capsule that would ride to space on a rocket launcher.

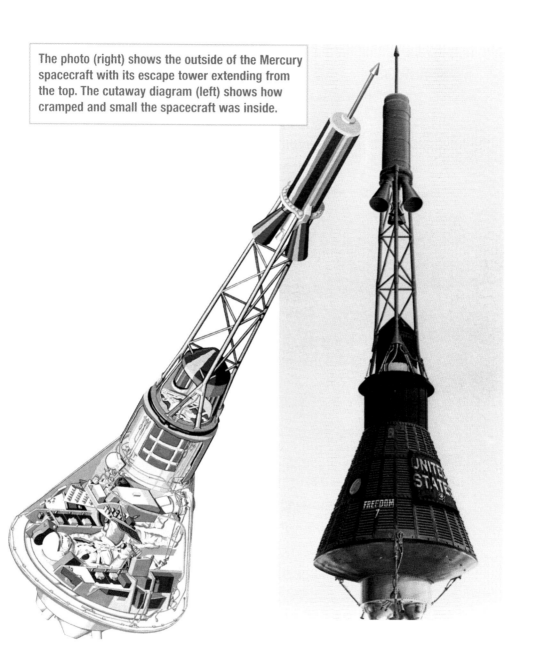

The photo (right) shows the outside of the Mercury spacecraft with its escape tower extending from the top. The cutaway diagram (left) shows how cramped and small the spacecraft was inside.

NASA had used the Viking rocket and the von Braun team's Juno rocket (also known as the Redstone rocket) to launch satellites, but both of these were medium-sized rockets. They did not have enough power to lob both a spacecraft and its pilot into orbit. So Mercury planners decided its first two missions would be *suborbital* flights powered by the Redstone rocket. These would take astronauts beyond Earth's atmosphere, but not into orbit.

For flights that orbited Earth, NASA eventually turned to an *intercontinental ballistic missile (ICBM)* named Atlas. The Atlas was a *multistage rocket.* That is, it had a main engine and two boosters. The Atlas was taller than the Redstone rocket and considerably bigger around. The Atlas stood 82.5 feet (25 m) tall and was 10 feet (3 m) in diameter. Without a *payload,* it weighed about 266,000 pounds (120,600 kg). At takeoff, the Atlas's two booster engines burned to assist the main engine. After 145 seconds, the boosters separated and the main engine lifted the rocket into space.

To reduce the rocket's weight, its designers had not used the usual thick outer covering and big supporting struts. Instead, they used a pressurized body with a skin so thin that some critics called it the "steel balloon." Von Braun thought it was unsafe, but the Atlas rocket designers invited him to take a sledge hammer to it. One engineer tried to put a hole in the Atlas skin, but the sledgehammer just bounced back.

Even so, early Atlas launch tests were not always promising. Later astronaut Deke Slayton said wryly, "I spent most of my time that year at [Cape Canaveral] watching Atlases take off and blow up." For someone who planned to travel into space aboard an Atlas, the experience must have been unsettling.

Shortly after he arrived in the United States, Wernher von Braun was surprised by some of the questions reporters asked him about rockets. He didn't understand why they didn't already know the answers. After all, the United States was home to one of the most renowned rocket pioneers in the world.

"Don't you know about your own rocket pioneer?" von Braun asked. "Dr. Goddard was ahead of us all."

The man now known as "the father of American rocketry," had avoided publicity for most of his career. In 1920, The *New York Times* had ridiculed him as the "Moon Man" for suggesting that one day a rocket might reach the Moon. The experience had discouraged the hardworking scientist from speaking to journalists.

Fascinated with rockets since his youth, Goddard was a hands-on engineer as well as a scientist and theorist. He began testing rockets in 1908, and by 1914 he had experimented with several types of rockets and a variety of fuels. More importantly, in 1915 he proved that rocket engines could produce thrust in a vacuum. Because space is a vacuum, this breakthrough confirmed that rockets could be used for space flight. Goddard launched his first liquid-fueled rocket in 1926.

However, neighbors in his small New England town raised such a commotion about the noise and explosions that he moved his testing range to New Mexico in 1929. There, with help from the Smithsonian Institution and the Guggenheim Foundation, he continued to develop his rockets. He worked on everything from combustion chambers to steering mechanisms.

In 1960, 15 years after Goddard's death, official recognition of his great contributions to rocket science finally came when the U.S. government paid $1 million to his estate for the legal right to more than 200 patents. NASA's Goddard Space Flight Center is named in his honor.

Robert Goddard standing by his 1926 liquid-fuel rocket

Stagecoach to Space

In the meantime, development went forward on designing a wingless spacecraft. It would carry a human passenger into space and return safely to Earth. The design had to protect the astronauts from the extremes of space—including very high and low temperatures, an airless environment, and radiation. It also had to reenter Earth's atmosphere without burning up.

NASA involved the astronauts directly in checking the design and production quality of the Mercury spacecraft. They all had high motivation as well as the technical expertise to troubleshoot potential problems effectively—and each one was responsible for particular parts of the system.

As Wally Schirra wrote in his book *Schirra's Space*, "My most beautiful memory of the Mercury Program is how seven men—all superachievers with super egos—came together to work as a team. We had total faith in one another . . . ."

The tiny cone-shaped Mercury capsule was barely big enough for one pilot. As a joke, John Glenn posted a warning in Alan Shepard's capsule, "NO HANDBALL PLAYING IN HERE." Shepard was lucky if he could wiggle his eyebrows.

Each astronaut traveled on his back, squeezed into the wide end of the cone. Each seat was custom-molded to fit its pilot. At liftoff, pressure equivalent to six times Earth's normal gravity would press the astronaut back into his seat. The custom molding made sure the pressure would be evenly distributed.

The Mercury spacesuit design mimicked the pressurized suit worn by U.S. Navy high-altitude jet-aircraft pilots. The inside layer was

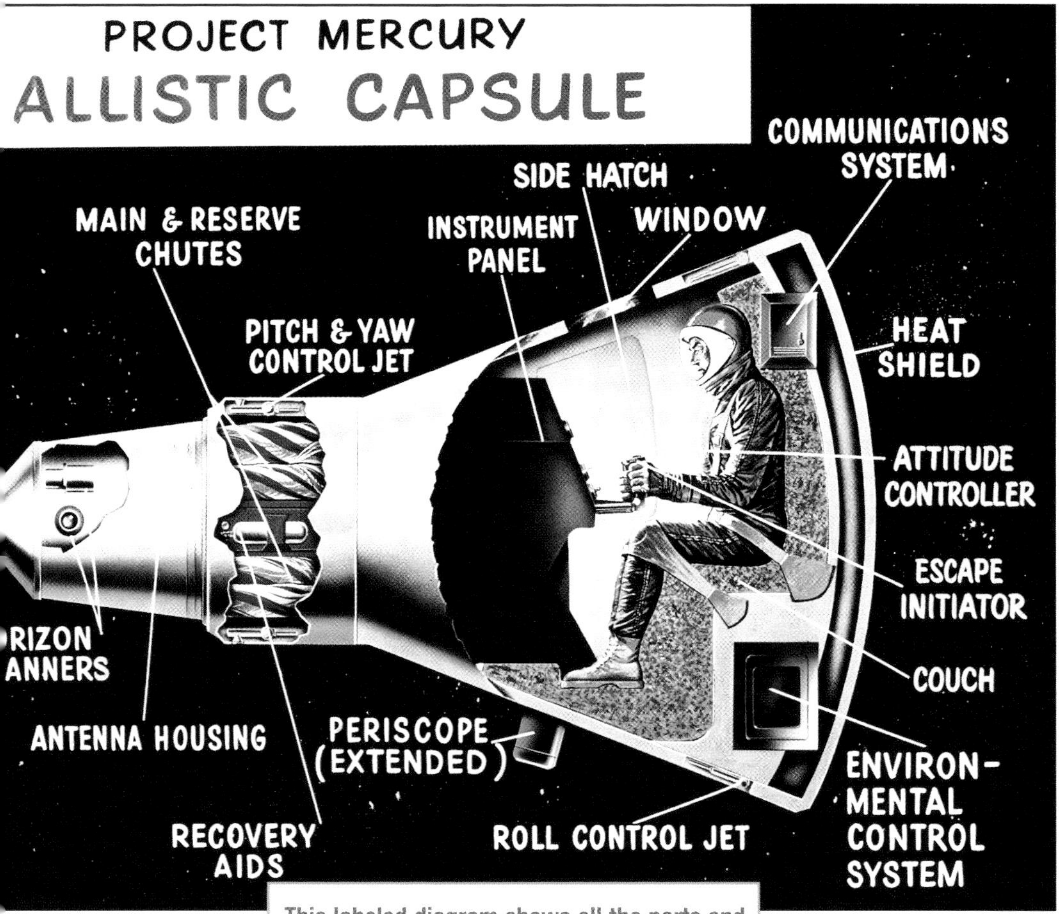

PROJECT MERCURY
ALLISTIC CAPSULE

COMMUNICATIONS SYSTEM·

SIDE HATCH ·

WINDOW

INSTRUMENT PANEL

MAIN & RESERVE CHUTES

PITCH & YAW CONTROL JET

HEAT SHIELD

ATTITUDE CONTROLLER

ESCAPE INITIATOR

RIZON ANNERS

COUCH

ANTENNA HOUSING

PERISCOPE (EXTENDED)

ENVIRON- MENTAL CONTROL SYSTEM

RECOVERY AIDS

ROLL CONTROL JET

This labeled diagram shows all the parts and equipment inside the Mercury capsule.

made of nylon with a special coating. The outside layer was made of aluminized nylon. The suit could bend at the joints, such as elbows or knees, but it was very stiff when pressurized. The Mercury cabin was pressurized, so the astronauts did not have to pressurize their suits during the entire flight. Pressure returned quickly to the suit when the helmet's visor was lowered.

A small window on one side of the capsule provided a limited view—but as the astronauts would soon find out, even a limited view from space can be spectacular. Overhead, the view from the periscope was displayed.

The control consoles were not much use. The astronaut could not really direct much more than the spacecraft's attitude. As former ace pilots, the Mercury astronauts were uncomfortable with the idea of traveling into space aboard a wingless capsule with so little control. Some people called the whole concept "Spam in a can"—a grim reference to being helpless chopped meat traveling in a craft no more manageable than a tin can.

During liftoff, though, the astronauts had an opportunity to escape if there was trouble. An escape tower above the capsule would pull the capsule and its pilot out of danger. Luckily, this feature was never needed.

The outside surface of the tiny Mercury spacecraft was constructed of nickel alloy covered with a thin layer of heat-resistant titanium. At the wide bottom of the cone-shaped spacecraft, a heat shield provided protection from the intense heat of reentry into Earth's atmosphere.

The Mercury capsule was small and uncomfortable, the window was tiny, and the astronauts had minimal control, but the little spacecraft worked—and it worked every time it flew. That was important, and that was the intention of its designers, led by a man named Max Faget.

Yuri Gets There First

By December 1960, NASA had made many tests, including the launch of an unpiloted Mercury capsule. This capsule made a suborbital flight—much like the one the first astronaut would make. Everything had been checked and re-checked.

In his autobiography *Deke!*, astronaut Deke Slayton describes Max Faget as "a feisty guy who came out of Louisiana and had served on submarines during World War II. He was a science-fiction reader, like a lot of engineers at that time, and [he] wasn't afraid to come up with something wild or new. Once he settled on a concept, that was it, too. He wasn't afraid to argue."

As one of the prime designers of the Mercury spacecraft, Faget had to do a lot of arguing. No one had ever really designed a piloted spacecraft before and people had different ideas about how to do it. The capsule had to be small, quick, safe, and light enough to be carried into orbit by a Redstone or Atlas missile. It also had to return the astronaut safely to Earth. Thanks to Max Faget's support, the cone-shaped capsule won out over other designs. Faget knew it was the safest way to go. The spacecraft needed a big, blunt bottom coated with a thick material to absorb heat during reentry. Max Faget's Mercury capsule was squat, small, and ugly—but it did the job.

Max Faget, spacecraft designer

The engineers wanted to be sure that an astronaut could escape using the escape tower if something went wrong during liftoff. They wanted to test the spacecraft's aerodynamics as well as its controls and computer systems. They wanted to make sure the heat shield would work during reentry. Most important of all, they wanted to be sure that the capsule would stay intact during splashdown, that the astronauts could emerge through the hatch, and that the recovery crews could rescue the astronauts from the cold ocean waters.

Engineers used simulated human pilots, wired to send back information from space, to verify the safety of liftoff, ascent, suborbital flight, and descent. Meanwhile, the ground crew and recovery teams were acquiring the experience of a dress rehearsal.

The last test for the first piloted flight took place in January 1961. This one carried a passenger, a chimpanzee named Ham. The test went very well, and Ham returned to Earth in excellent health.

NASA still wasn't quite ready to send an astronaut into space, though. Even though Ham had done well on his test flight, Wernher von Braun still had some concerns. The Redstone rocket didn't accelerate perfectly and it vibrated too much. Von Braun wanted a flawless flight. The life of an astronaut was at stake, and so was the reputation of the nation. He insisted on one more test.

A Redstone carrying an unpiloted Mercury capsule made the test flight in March, and it went perfectly. The next Redstone would carry an astronaut, and the flight was scheduled for May. But then the Soviets did it again.

On April 12, 1961, just as Project Mercury was warming up for its first piloted launch, the news came in: The Soviet Union had sent a man into space. Yuri Gagarin, an air force jet pilot from a small town near Moscow had soared into space from a Soviet launch site in Kazakhstan. He made one complete orbit of Earth and landed safely near the Volga River. The trip lasted almost 2 hours, and the effect was sensational. The world would never forget this moment.

Soviet cosmonaut Yuri Gagarin, the first human to orbit Earth

Not until 1995 did notes from Gagarin's commander reveal that the last moments of the flight were frighteningly perilous. The braking rocket, which slowed Gagarin's spacecraft, malfunctioned. The spacecraft and the attached rocket began twisting wildly. Also, the rocket did not separate as soon as it should have, and even when it did, the spacecraft continued to careen. Luckily, the Soviet spacecraft came equipped with an ejector seat and parachute for the cosmonaut's landing. The ejector seat worked well, and Gagarin parachuted safely to the ground. The first human voyage to space was a success.

The Soviet space program had scored another big coup, and the U.S. program was clearly struggling. The tension grew as NASA prepared to send the first U.S. astronaut into space.

Chapter 4

Venturing into Space

Some critics have pointed out that if the March test had carried an astronaut, the United States, not the Soviet Union, would have been the first to put a man in space. Yet, von Braun's caution was one of the mainstays of the U.S. space program's success. He and his engineering team insisted on systems that worked, and they built "redundancy" into their designs. That is, in case a part did not work properly during flight, the engineers included a back-up part or another method of accomplishing the same task. Their meticulous and thorough approach cost money and time, but it removed unnecessary dangers from what has always been a risky business.

After the perfectly executed March flight, the Redstone-Mercury duo had von Braun's seal of approval. It was ready for its first astronaut.

German-born engineer Wernher von Braun was key to the success of the U.S. space program.

Shepard for the Job

Alan Shepard, at 35, was selected for the job. His fellow astronauts thought of him as the one who could see the big picture. He understood how the details fit together to make things work. He also observed carefully and always offered insights. They nicknamed him "professor" because of the serious way he answered questions at press conferences—with responses full of many, often dry, details.

Now he was the one selected by NASA and the other astronauts to try out the new spacecraft first. He very much wanted the job. Before the selection, he said, "There are lots of answers why I want to be the first man in space, but a short answer would be this: The flight obviously is a challenge and I feel that the more severe challenge will occur on the first flight and I signed up to accept this challenge."

At 5 feet 11 inches (180 cm), Shepard was the tallest of the Mercury Seven. The Mercury capsule was only 10 feet (3 m) high and a little more than 6 feet (1.8 m) wide at the base. It practically took a shoehorn to get Shepard into the capsule. Once he connected his spacesuit up for all the monitoring the NASA scientists wanted to do, he could barely move anything but his eyeballs.

He also had one added piece of equipment that the rest of the Mercury astronauts would not have, a parachute stored on a ledge inside the capsule cabin. Of course, it would be useless in the weightlessness and airlessness of space. It could only be helpful when Shepard returned to Earth's atmosphere—after the main parachute had opened and slowed his spacecraft. Then, if something went wrong, administrators had reasoned, he could jump and use the parachute. However, he would have to reach for the parachute, attach it to himself, maneuver to the hatch, open it, and make his way out—all the while plummeting toward Earth. In reality, the parachute was useless and just got in the way, so after *Freedom 7*'s flight, the astronauts left it on the ground.

The Day Arrives

For Alan Shepard, the morning of May 5, 1961, began at 1:10 A.M. The ground crew and operations team had been up all night at Cape Canaveral, Florida, preparing for the launch. Now they continued through the early hours of the morning, as they proceeded with the early stages of the countdown. Each step in the count involved an elaborate system of checks and final details.

Shepard, meanwhile, showered, shaved, and ate a hearty breakfast of orange juice, filet mignon wrapped in bacon, and scrambled eggs. An official pre-flight physical examination followed, and *biosensors* (electrodes to track heartbeat, breathing, and other body functions)

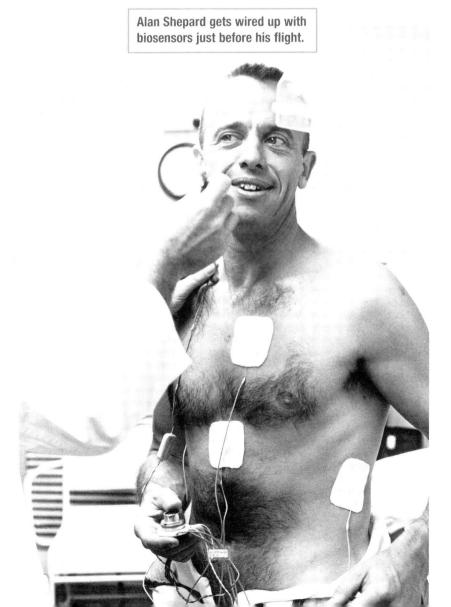

Alan Shepard gets wired up with biosensors just before his flight.

In the beginning, no one really knew what would happen to the human body in space. Would a person's body systems be able to function in an environment without gravity? "There was a lot of doubt," Shepard remarked 30 years later, " . . . especially from some of the more learned members of the medical community who thought a man shouldn't be in space; it wasn't his place to be there."

NASA physicians and scientists wanted detailed reports for every moment of every journey. Could the digestive system function without the familiar tug of gravity? How would the cardiovascular system react to weightlessness? Some scientists feared that the eyeballs would bulge without the presence of air pressure and gravity. Zero-g might create inner-ear problems, too, causing extreme nausea and disorientation. If an astronaut caught a cold, how would he blow his nose?

Early astronauts wore wired electrodes that reported their physical condition to Mission Control. The astronauts also underwent physical exams before and after each mission. Scientists wanted to measure what happened to muscles and bone and brain cells.

Today, scientists continue to study the effects of extended exposure to zero gravity. Some crews have conducted long-duration missions of more than a year—and some visionaries look forward to sending astronauts to Mars.

were attached to his body. During flight, these biosensors would allow the NASA medical team to monitor Shepard's health as well as his physical reactions to the unknown effects of space. How would his body hold up in zero-g—the absence of gravity? Then a technician helped Shepard put on the spacesuit that would protect him if his capsule lost pressure.

At 3:55 A.M., it was time for Shepard to board the van that would take him out to the launchpad where the slender 69-foot (21-m) Redstone rocket stood, nearly ready for liftoff. The launch vehicle was about as tall as a five-story building. The little Mercury capsule and its escape tower were mounted on top. "The large majority of the population thought we were crazy sitting on top of a rocket and allowing ourselves to be thrust into space," Shepard recalled years later.

Not a moment was wasted. As soon as Shepard arrived at the pad, technicians attached his gloves, while fellow astronaut Gordon Cooper brought him up to date on the status of the launch so far. At 5:15 A.M., Shepard went up the gantry—the massive scaffold-like structure that extended skyward alongside the rocket from the ground to the capsule. Five minutes later, he was climbing into the spacecraft. He eased down into the couch that would be his home in space. He fit snugly inside the frail little capsule he had named *Freedom 7*.

It was still 2 hours and 5 minutes until liftoff. A technician attached hoses and the seat harness to Shepard, and then shook the astronaut's hand as the gantry crew waved with a jubilant, "Happy landings, Commander!" From here on out, it would be just one person, Alan Shepard, alone against the unknowns of space. As the hatch closed, Shepard's heart pounded for a moment. Then, professional to the core, he quickly regained his usual calm.

At 6:25 A.M., Shepard began breathing pure oxygen to prevent decompression sickness, or the "bends," as divers call it. He was ready now. The countdown, which had halted to give him time to get settled, started again. It was 15 minutes before liftoff.

Then a hold was called to wait 35 to 40 minutes for the weather to clear. The minutes ticked by. Then another hold was called to replace a part in the Redstone's electrical system. That took nearly an hour, and the countdown was restarted at liftoff minus 35 minutes. Then there was another frustrating hold. This time a key computer at Goddard Space Center in Maryland was malfunctioning. It took another 2 hours and 34 minutes to set it right.

Finally the countdown restarted. Shepard's wait time in the capsule before liftoff totaled 4 hours and 14 minutes. That caused another glitch in the process. Apparently, no one had thought about how the astronauts would relieve themselves, and after all this waiting, Shepard's bladder was full. Von Braun wouldn't let him leave the capsule, and so Shepard decided to take care of the problem where he was. He did, and the countdown resumed.

Into Space

This time, the countdown went smoothly, and things really began to gear up. Voice communications switched from Gordon Cooper in the blockhouse to the Mercury Control Center, where Deke Slayton began relaying each system's monitor readouts to Shepard in the capsule. Overhead, Wally Schirra was circling in his F-106 chase plane, waiting. He would follow Shepard as high as he could.

As liftoff neared, Shepard's heartbeat stepped up, and so did the heartbeats of his fellow astronauts, the ground crew, the press corps attending the launch, and the millions of people watching the historic event on television. This was the moment everyone in the United States had been waiting for.

The electrical connection to the outside world fell away, the Redstone thundered, and a cloud of smoke billowed up. Liftoff was smooth and even, and Slayton's voice came through loud and clear. Shepard replied calmly, "Ahh, Roger; liftoff and the clock has started . . . Yes, sir, reading you loud and clear. This is *Freedom 7*. The fuel is go. Cabin at fourteen [pounds per square inch pressure]. Oxygen is go. . . . *Freedom 7* is still go."

Freedom 7, with Alan Shepard aboard, begins its historic suborbital flight.

As the spacecraft's speed reached the speed of sound, the rocket and capsule began to tremble, but Shepard had trained for this and knew what to expect. About 88 seconds after liftoff, the vibrations became so rough that Shepard couldn't hold his head still to read the dials on his panels. The thundering increased. Two minutes after launch he felt the press of more than six times Earth's gravity as the rocket's acceleration pressed him heavily into his custom-fitted couch.

Then, at an altitude of 116.5 miles (187 km) above Earth's surface, the engines cut off on schedule, and the rocket dropped away. He could hear the small rocket fire that *jettisoned* the escape tower. The green light on his control panel told him it had dropped away. Outside, the temperature registered 220 degrees Fahrenheit (104 degrees Celsius). Inside the capsule, though, the temperature was a much more moderate 91°F (33°C), and inside Shepard's spacesuit was a comfortable 75°F (24°C).

Alan Shepard and *Freedom 7* were on their own, hurtling through space at more than 5,000 miles (8,047 km) per hour. He was a scant 1 degree off course. Three minutes after liftoff, the automatic attitude control system came on and positioned the capsule with its broad-base heat shield flying forward. As *Freedom 7* moved toward the peak of its arc, Shepard set to work on the key purpose of his mission—demonstrating whether an astronaut could control a spacecraft in space. If he couldn't, all the plans for the Mercury Project—and, quite possibly, the entire future of humans in space—could be in jeopardy.

Shepard switched the controls from automatic to manual, one at a time, carefully testing each one. First he tried *pitch*, the forward-back angle of the spacecraft. *Freedom 7* was automatically set at 45 degrees.

Now Shepard changed it to 34 degrees, which more recent studies showed would work better. He set the other controls to manual, as well, and found that they worked smoothly.

Next he conducted some limited observations through the periscope. He could make out continental landmasses. Even though he was looking through a gray filter left accidentally in place, he could distinguish land from clouds, and he could recognize the Gulf of Mexico and the Florida coast along the Gulf. Lake Okeechobee in central Florida also came into view as well as the Bahamas. Shepard had practiced sighting these landmasses during training.

Splashdown

Before Shepard could do much more, his 15-minute trip began to wind down. He heard the retrorockets fire to slow the craft as it arced downward toward the water. Shepard used hydrogen peroxide jets to adjust the attitude. He was pleased at how well they worked.

As he plunged Earthward, Shepard was subjected to almost 12-g forces, twice what he had endured on liftoff. The descent seemed more rapid than he expected, and he was worried because the small parachute had not yet popped to slow the spacecraft. Finally, at about 21,000 feet (6,401 m), the parachute opened. It was a huge relief to Shepard, but, actually, that's about when it was supposed to open.

When *Freedom 7* reached 10,000 feet (3,050 m), the main parachute popped open, further slowing the capsule. A few moments later, *Freedom 7* hit the water, tilted, and then righted itself, bobbing like a big, charred cork. It was the first piloted "splashdown" from space, and it went perfectly.

From NASA administrators to fellow astronauts to millions of people watching on television—everyone felt the elation of success. Legend has it that Shepard declared, "Everything is A-OK!" right after his landing, as his capsule still floated in the Atlantic. If he didn't, he certainly could have—because everything had gone just as planned. In any case, newspaper reporters picked it up as astronaut talk for "everything is all right," and "A-OK" soon became a permanent addition to American speech.

The splashdown was a uniquely American method of reentry. Gagarin and all the Vostok cosmonauts after him parachuted out of their spacecraft from an altitude of 20,013 feet (6,100 m), leaving the spacecraft to plummet to Earth on its own. Shepard had landed 65 miles (105 km) from Bermuda, right on target. As he climbed through the hatch and slipped into the waters of the Atlantic Ocean, a Marine Corps helicopter fished Shepard and his spacecraft from the water and carried them to the recovery ship, the aircraft carrier *Lake Champlain*.

From liftoff to splashdown, Alan Shepard's mission had lasted just 15 minutes. He had reached an altitude of 116.5 miles (187 km). The total distance of his mission was 302 miles (486 km). Shepard had spent only about 5 minutes outside Earth's atmosphere, but he had accomplished all his objectives—and more.

The Mercury Project had placed a human in space, and he had survived. As Shepard told the medical team who examined him immediately after the flight, "It was painless. Just a pleasant ride." That was significant. Before 1961, no one knew whether humans could endure high gravity loads and weightlessness without physical or mental damage. Shepard had also executed his tasks well and maintained his cool.

A Marine Corps helicopter recovers astronaut Alan Shepard and *Freedom 7* after splashdown in the Atlantic Ocean.

Alan Shepard had always loved flying. When he was a kid, he used to ride his bicycle 10 miles (16 km) to a nearby airport. There, he bartered odd jobs for free rides on the airplanes. After serving aboard a destroyer in World War II, Shepard became a Navy test pilot for fighter jets and pioneered landing techniques on angled-deck aircraft carriers.

He was 35 when he became an astronaut, and he still flew every chance he got. He also loved to race his white Corvette.

After his *Freedom 7* flight, Shepard developed an inner-ear disorder. For the next decade, the condition kept him from flying in space. But after the problem was corrected by surgery, he received his second assignment. Traveling with Edgar Mitchell and Stuart Roosa, he went to the Moon as commander of *Apollo 14* in 1971. Shepard and Mitchell descended to the Moon's surface in the lunar lander *Antares*, landing in the Fra Mauro uplands.

The two astronauts explored the edge of a crater and collected 94.3 pounds (42.8 kg) of rocks during two *extravehicular activities (EVAs)*—hikes outside the spacecraft. While he was there, Shepard demonstrated the Moon's gravity to television viewers by hitting a golf ball. The ball sailed far from sight in gravity only one-sixth Earth's gravity. Alan Shepard was the only Mercury astronaut to walk on the Moon.

Shepard had a keen interest in private enterprise, which he pursued avidly throughout his career. Even before his retirement he had become a millionaire, and after retirement, he devoted all his energies to his business interests, which included banks, oil wells, real estate, and quarter horses. Alan Shepard died on July 22, 1998, of leukemia. He was 74.

Alan Shepard standing next to a lunar training vehicle in 1970

After so much loss of face against the Soviets, American spirits lifted with pride.

President John F. Kennedy was enormously pleased and telephoned his congratulations to the triumphant astronaut aboard the recovery ship. The next day, Kennedy gave Alan Shepard the Medal of Distinguished Service in a special ceremony in the White House Rose Garden. Two days after his landing, a crowd of 250,000 people cheered Shepard at a parade in Washington, D.C.

Aiming for the Moon

The United States had put a human being in space, and Alan Shepard was an undisputed hero. Because Yuri Gagarin had achieved orbit and stayed in space for 108 minutes, Shepard's flight seemed less ambitious to some. But Shepard was the first pilot to have any control of his spacecraft in space. To the U.S. astronauts, this distinction seemed critical—after all, a less-automated spacecraft required more skill from its pilot.

As far as NASA was concerned, a pilot could adapt more quickly to changing circumstances than a computer program. Also, a piloted spacecraft would have more versatility. As a result, the U.S. space program would always rely less on computerized navigation than the Soviet program did.

Less than 3 weeks after Shepard's flight, President Kennedy made an announcement that caught both the spirit and the imagination of the American people. He declared: "I believe that this nation should commit itself to achieving the goal, before this decade is out, of landing a man on the Moon and returning him safely to the earth."

President John F. Kennedy's plan to send an astronaut to the Moon set a heroic goal for the United States.

The moment was right, and Congress put up little objection to the giant undertaking. Newspapers, magazines, and television endorsed it heartily. The United States was headed for the Moon. The announcement set a new tone for Project Mercury.

Emergency at Sea

Not everything went as smoothly, though, for the next mission. Gus Grissom took the second Mercury spacecraft, *Liberty Bell 7*, into a similar suborbital flight in July 1961. As he lowered himself into the spacecraft, he seemed calm and in command. Since Shepard's flight, some improvements had been made to the Mercury capsule. One of these was a new, larger window that gave the pilot a better view of the horizon, landmasses, and the surroundings of the spacecraft. NASA had also added a urinal system.

Overall, most of Grissom's flight seemed uneventful—although physical monitors noted occasional rapid heartbeats, and Grissom later confessed to being "a bit scared" at liftoff, as the powerful rocket lunged upward. Grissom was amazed at the sights he could see from the spacecraft. At the peak of his ascent, he could see an 800-mile (1,288-km) arc of Earth's horizon. He tried to report all the landmarks he saw and, in the process, fell a little behind in his tasks.

However, most of the return trip went smoothly. The parachutes opened on time, and *Liberty Bell 7* dropped into the ocean. Then, trouble began. Deep swells moved across the ocean surface, and the capsule tipped all the way over on its side. But the capsule slowly bobbed upright so that Grissom could see above the water line out the window. Everything seemed airtight.

The rescue helicopters radioed Grissom that they were coming in to pick him up, and, after making some log notes, he lay back in the couch. As he later declared, "I was lying there, minding my own business, when I heard a dull thud." The hatch detonators (small explosives that open the hatch) had blown! The hatch streaked away from the capsule. The helicopter crew watched the hatch skip across the waves as if it had been shot from a rifle. Grissom quickly realized that *Liberty Bell 7* was taking on water from the ocean's heavy swells. The capsule was about to sink—with him onboard! He quickly took off his helmet, tried to adjust the inflatable collar on his suit, and struggled out of the sloshing hatch. He dived into the cold water and signaled frantically for the helicopter to pick him up.

The helicopter crew saw Grissom waving his hands for help, but mistook his signals. They thought he meant he was all right, so they concentrated on trying to pull the capsule out of the water. They succeeded in attaching their hoist cable to the *Liberty Bell,* but it was full of water and sinking quickly. As it sank toward the ocean bottom, it pulled the helicopter with it, until the rescue craft was touching the wave tops. The helicopter kept tugging, but the spacecraft acted like a water-filled anchor. With the water it had taken on, *Liberty Bell 7* weighed more than 5,000 pounds (2,270 kg)—about 1,000 pounds (454 kg) more than the helicopter could lift. Finally, the crew realized that the engine was overworking and in danger of failing. They let the spacecraft go.

Liberty Bell 7 sank to the ocean floor. It was the only spacecraft lost on splashdown during all the Mercury, Gemini, and Apollo missions.

Grissom, meanwhile, was close to drowning. The air in his collar was escaping, and he was having trouble treading water in his heavy spacesuit. Finally, a second helicopter crew fished him out of the water and took him to the recovery ship, where he tried to reconstruct what happened. During the next few months, the hatch manufacturer, closely monitored by astronaut Wally Schirra, made extensive, rigorous tests to see what might have caused the hatch to blow off. NASA officials were never able to figure out exactly what had happened, but they

A U.S. Marine Corps helicopter attempting to lift *Liberty Bell 7* from the Atlantic Ocean.

Gus Grissom was the only one of the Mercury Seven who did not live to see the first astronaut step on the Moon. An ace astronaut, he played key roles in both the Mercury and the Gemini programs, and he was Commander of *Apollo 1*.

Four years after his Mercury flight, Grissom flew a solid mission with astronaut John Young in the first piloted Gemini mission (*Gemini 3*), which Grissom dubbed *Molly Brown* in memory of his sunken *Liberty Bell 7*. (*The Unsinkable Molly Brown*, about a survivor of the sinking of the *Titanic*, was a popular Broadway musical at the time.) The mission went well.

The original Apollo command module (CM) had design flaws, though, and Grissom was always outspoken about them. As a joke, he hung a lemon on the *Apollo 1* CM—his way of showing his low opinion. The gesture came to have a terrible irony.

On January 27, 1967, Grissom and his crewmates Ed White and Roger Chaffee boarded the *Apollo 1* command module for a routine test. Suddenly, a fire broke out inside the cabin. A ground crew member rushed to help, but explosive flames forced him back. From inside, the three crew members struggled to open the door, but they couldn't. Within seconds, all three died of asphyxiation.

Fellow astronauts remembered Grissom as shy, snarly, and tough. He was a highly trained astronaut, a top pilot, and an excellent engineer. In 1997, the *Apollo 1* crew was awarded the Congressional Space Medal of Honor. It was the thirtieth anniversary of the fire.

Gus Grissom (left) and John Young (right) in training for their *Gemini 3* mission

did not lose confidence in Grissom. He was later selected to command two other missions. New safety standards were set for the hatch, and the accident never happened again.

In 1999, a space museum in Kansas teamed up with a specialized salvage crew to rescue Gus Grissom's spacecraft. Nearly 38 years after

Liberty Bell 7 after its recovery in 1999

its loss, it was raised from the ocean floor about 90 miles (140 km) northeast of Great Abaco Island in the Bahamas. It came up in one piece and now resides at the Kansas Cosmosphere and Space Center in Hutchinson, Kansas. There visitors can watch curators working to restore the capsule.

Chapter 5

Orbit at Last!

If you looked at it one way, the two suborbital flights by Shepard and Grissom seemed to put the United States solidly ahead in the space race—Soviet Union 1: United States 2.

Yet, some space watchers pointed out that Shepard's and Grissom's flights had not reached Earth orbit. Yuri Gagarin's flight had entered orbit and was more than three times longer than both U.S. flights together.

Then, within a month, the pressure was really on again. On August 6, 1961, the Soviet Union launched *Vostok 2* with cosmonaut Gherman Titov aboard. Titov spent more than 2 days—25 hours and 18 minutes—in space and completed 17 Earth orbits.

Soviet cosmonaut Gherman Titov

Original plans for the Mercury Project had called for each astronaut to make one suborbital flight before making any orbital flights. Now all those plans were scrapped. The time had come to place an American in orbit.

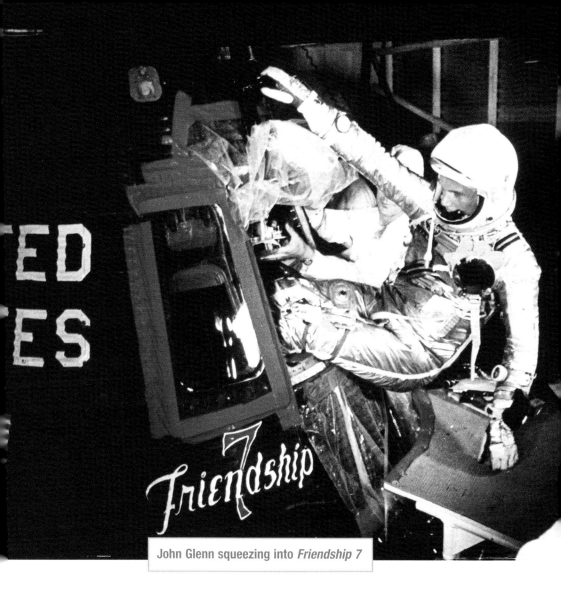

John Glenn squeezing into *Friendship 7*

More Rocket Power

To lift a spacecraft and astronaut into orbit, though, NASA needed a bigger rocket. However, early tests of the Atlas rocket had gone badly—two out of five unmanned tests had failed—and the big rocket had problems carrying the Mercury spacecraft. Thirty-five years later, the memory of one nighttime Atlas test still resonated strongly for astronaut John Glenn, who recalled the launch site lit by searchlights beneath a starry sky. All was ready. Then, he said, "They light this thing, and up she goes . . . At about 27,000 feet it blew up right over our heads. It looked like an atom bomb went off right there."

John Glenn had a special reason for concern. As the most experienced pilot, he had been chosen to make the first orbital flight atop that same undependable rocket. Originally scheduled for liftoff in December 1961, Glenn's mission was canceled nine times for various reasons, including bad weather and continuing problems with the rocket. Finally, though, the tests succeeded, and the big day came. Seven months had passed since the last U.S. spaceflight.

Launch to Orbit

On February 20, 1962, the Atlas rocket lifted off, carrying John Glenn aboard the Mercury capsule *Friendship 7*. Speeding at 17,500 miles (28,164 km) per hour, Glenn reached orbit and began his first revolution around the planet. On the way he could see the curving edge of Earth's horizon against the black night of space. The sights he reported from this vantage in space were stunning—piles of clouds, dust storms in Africa, and a sensational sunset.

"Orbital sunset is tremendous," he said, ". . . a truly beautiful, beautiful sight." He saw the horizon's white light caught between the dark night on Earth and the blackness of space. "As the Sun goes down a little bit more," he continued, "the bottom layer becomes orange, and it fades into red and finally off into blues and black as you look farther up into space."

By the end of that day in space, Glenn would see not one, but four sunsets—three from Earth orbit and one after splashdown. Looking back some 35 years later, he recalled the beauty of a sunset in space.

John Glenn took this view of Earth from *Friendship 7.*

"Here on Earth you see a sunset, it's golden, it's orange," he said. In space, though, it "has the same glowing color for all the colors of the spectrum . . ."

Glenn was traveling fast, moving backward—as all Mercury spacecraft did. Seven orbits looked like a good bet at the outset. He checked his controls and systems. Then, as he soared over Australia, he saw a strange sight. "I'm in a big mass of some very small particles that are brilliantly lit up," he radioed his communications link, "like they're luminescent. . . . there are literally thousands of them!" These "fireflies," as he called them, were mysterious, but apparently harmless, and the mission continued.

Then a problem with the automatic attitude-control system developed. Under automatic control, the spacecraft began drifting. Glenn had to adjust the attitude manually to make up for the drifting.

Meanwhile, controllers on the ground became worried about a more serious problem. Their instruments showed that the landing bag had deployed early in the flight. This could mean that *Friendship 7*'s heat shield had come loose. If so, Glenn was in grave danger. Without the heat shield, he would burn up in Earth's atmosphere.

The situation now looked dangerous. Mission control instructed Glenn to complete only three orbits.

Rough Landing

The ground controllers also told Glenn to keep the spacecraft's retrorockets in place after they fired at the end of his flight. Ordinarily they were jettisoned, or discarded, but maybe the straps that attached them to the spacecraft would help to hold the heat shield in place during reentry.

Max Faget, who had designed the spacecraft, agreed that this plan might work. Aerodynamics should keep the whole thing in place once reentry began, he said, even if the straps burned off. If any of the retrorockets did not fire, though, he cautioned, they would have to be jettisoned. Otherwise, they would definitely explode during reentry, and John Glenn would be blown to bits.

As Glenn started back through the atmosphere, a fireball streaked in front of his window. He thought it was either the retrorockets or the heat shield—and he knew if his heat shield was flying by, his mission was over. It turned out to be just a piece of the retrorockets that had broken loose after firing. The heat shield was intact and did its job.

Even before becoming an astronaut, John Glenn had shown both courage and skill. He flew 149 combat missions in World War II and the Korean War. He also earned the Distinguished Flying Cross five times and won nineteen Air Medals. In 1957, he averaged supersonic speeds—despite inflight refueling—in a record-breaking flight from New York to Los Angeles that took only 3 hours and 23 minutes.

Glenn was 37 when he became an astronaut, the oldest of the Mercury Seven. He had wisdom about practical matters of influence and image, and he managed his own image well. He had an easygoing, charismatic personality that was unusual among test pilots, who are often loners with intense personalities. He also liked to cultivate the "all-American" Boy-Scout image that NASA encour-

aged in astronauts. His fellow astronauts remember him as a man with a bigger mission—a desire to make the world a better place—even then.

Three years after his famous *Friendship 7* spaceflight, John Glenn retired from NASA for a new career. Glenn hoped to use his high profile to gain political office. He became a U.S. senator from Ohio in 1974 and was easily reelected to the Senate three times. He retired from politics in 1998.

In October 1998, John Glenn returned to space once more—this time as a member of the Space Shuttle crew of the orbiter *Discovery*. NASA used his flight to study the effects of weightlessness on an older person, but it was also an honorary tribute to a great space pioneer. He was 77 years old, the oldest human to go into space.

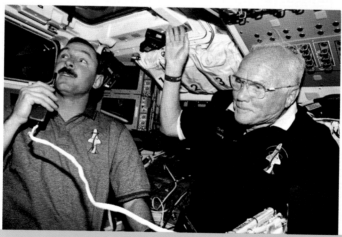

John Glenn (right) with mission commander Curtis L. Brown (left) aboard the Space Shuttle *Discovery* in 1998

The ground-control instruments were wrong, and John Glenn splashed down northeast of Puerto Rico exactly as planned.

Glenn's flight had lasted 4 hours, 55 minutes, and 23 seconds—a fast way to spend 3 days, he joked. Glenn was treated to a hero's welcome, including a wild and joyous ticker-tape parade in New York City. It was Glenn's turn now to make world headlines, and the United States regained some of its lost prestige in the space race. The space program was truly underway.

Chapter 6

The Last Three Missions

The first three Mercury missions had met NASA's basic goals. Now, in the missions remaining, Project Mercury would extend the astronauts' experience. They would explore the demands of space, experience longer missions, and continue learning to control a spacecraft. They would also have time to make observations that can only be made in space, viewing the world from above.

The next mission had been announced as Deke Slayton's. Although a minor heart murmur had kept him out of the running until now, the medical team had cleared him for flight at last. He was delighted, and well qualified for the job—an excellent flier who had talked the other astronauts through their missions. He had kept himself ready to go. Now it looked as if his chance had come.

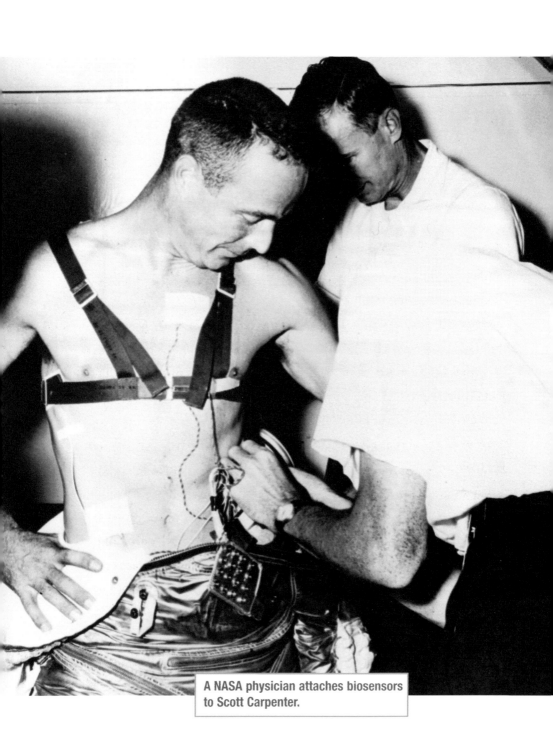

A NASA physician attaches biosensors to Scott Carpenter.

However, politics intervened. A White House science adviser insisted that if anything happened to Slayton, NASA funding could be reduced or cut off. The risk was too great, he claimed. Critics would say the agency shouldn't have taken the chance of losing both a spacecraft and an astronaut's life. NASA administrators fought the decision, but finally gave in and assigned John Glenn's backup—Scott Carpenter—instead. Slayton was tough, but his disappointment was keen.

Scary Splashdown

Carpenter's job was to repeat John Glenn's mission, almost exactly—making three orbits, testing the controls, making decisions about manual versus automated procedures, and performing a checklist of experiments.

Of all the Mercury Seven astronauts, Carpenter is often called the poet—observant, curious, and eloquent. He also may have been easily distracted. If NASA had noticed this tendency at the outset, Carpenter probably would not have become one of the Mercury Seven. NASA was looking for people who could maintain internal balance and think clearly under pressure.

The agency wanted astronauts who could work with machinelike precision and keep their minds on all the priorities and details. Some historians argue that Carpenter, who later became a writer, may have been overcome by the aesthetic experience of spaceflight when NASA needed him to keep his mind on flying his spacecraft. Actually, though, he may have just had an unlucky ride.

The morning was foggy as Carpenter arrived at Pad 14, where *Aurora 7* sat atop the 82.5-foot (25-m) Atlas rocket. The fog would lift shortly, though, the weather forecaster assured him. Carpenter

Astronaut Scott Carpenter in training for his Mercury mission

ascended the gantry and, after a few last-minute checks, he pulled his lean body into the capsule and settled onto the couch. A few moments later, the ground crew fastened the hatch bolts outside.

The countdown went smoothly, and only the fog appeared to present a problem. Meanwhile, Carpenter checked his preflight list. Finally, as the Sun rose, the fog vanished, and at 7:45 A.M. *Aurora 7* began liftoff as some 40 million people watched on television.

As Carpenter moved toward the blackness of space, he could see the sky getting darker. When the time came for the spacecraft to turn its heat shield to forward position, Carpenter elected to make the maneuver manually, since the automatic system had cost Glenn a lot of fuel during his flight. The maneuver went well, and Carpenter used only about one-third of the fuel Glenn had used.

Then he ran into a few difficulties. A control readout was incorrect on the panel, but he didn't notice it right away. Carpenter also had trouble getting film in his camera, setting him behind on other work he needed to do. When he tried out the controls, he probably used more fuel than he should have because the views of Earth were so stunning. Flight control told him to lay off the sightseeing and conserve fuel.

Unfortunately, while the spacecraft was on automatic, Carpenter accidentally turned on the manual thruster system for attitude control. As a result, both the automatic and the manual systems were running simultaneously—using twice as much fuel as normal. The switch was much too easy to turn on in zero-g, as Carpenter would later point out. Still, some 10 minutes went by before Carpenter noticed the problem. By the end of *Aurora 7*'s second orbit, mission control could see that the fuel supply had dropped to a dangerously low level. Orders came through to Carpenter: Use no more fuel until it is time for *retrofire*.

Carpenter provided glowing descriptions of what he saw. As he made his third orbit, he photographed the strange phenomenon of the flattened Sun at sunset. In all, he took nineteen photographs. Atmospheric scientists had told Carpenter that the images could be helpful in understanding the characteristics of the upper atmosphere. Carpenter's verbal description of the sunset was vivid as he crossed the Indian Ocean:

> The sunsets are most spectacular. The earth is black after the Sun has set. . . . The first band close to the earth is red, the next is yellow, the next is blue, the next is green, and the next is sort of a—sort of a purple. It's almost like a very brilliant rainbow. These layers extend from at least 90 degrees either side of the Sun at sunset.

During his third orbit, Carpenter told Slayton, who was on communications at the tracking position in Australia: ". . . the haze layer is very bright. . . . about twice as high above the horizon as the bright blue band at sunset is . . . ."

Scott Carpenter also saw the "fireflies" John Glenn had seen, and he performed a little experiment to find out more about them. Obviously, they weren't really fireflies, so what were they? He discovered that when he hit the interior of the capsule wall, the "fireflies" swarmed around outside the window. He tried it again and they swarmed again.

Carpenter knew he was low on fuel for the thrusters, but he was curious. When he fired the jets to turn the capsule around, he saw vapor that had vented from the spacecraft. He realized the venting was done to dispose of perspiration from his own body, and it was crystallizing as it flew by his window. The firefly mystery was solved.

The discovery took time, though, and Carpenter fell behind in preparing for the retrofire. Also, he realized that the problem he had with the control reading meant that the automatic system couldn't be used for retrofire. He would have to use the manual control. However, he couldn't quite get ready in time, and the retrofire took place 3 seconds later than scheduled.

As a result, Carpenter overshot his splashdown site by 250 miles (402 km), and he caused NASA major concern. Both he and his spacecraft could easily have been lost at sea. Luckily, search aircraft picked up

Scott Carpenter, being lifted to safety after splashing down 250 miles (402 km) from his planned landing area his radio beacon quickly. What happened? Fellow astronauts have said that Carpenter lost his cool and got too distracted by the view. Ground controllers had to remind him of his scheduled experiments all along the way. A controller at the Hawaii tracking station reported, "We had the impression he was very confused about what was going on. But it was very difficult to say whether he was confused or preoccupied."

Carpenter fluffed routine maneuvers performed easily by John Glenn, and he wasted considerable fuel when he accidentally turned on the backup thruster system. At the end of his mission, Carpenter was short of the fuel needed to correct his orientation. When it was time for retrofire, the capsule was not aligned correctly for landing. Carpenter also fired the retrorockets late. It was only about a 3-second delay, but the result was a big error when he landed.

Any one of these problems alone would not have caused much difficulty, but together they spelled trouble. On top of that, one of the Navy frogmen who helped rescue Carpenter told him that at first no one knew where he was. So, when a reporter on the carrier asked, Carpenter remarked, "I didn't know where I was, and they didn't either." He thought it was true.

Of course it wasn't true, but the astronaut's offhanded comment made NASA look incompetent. Flight Director Chris Kraft swore that Carpenter would never go into space again as long as Kraft had anything to do with it. It was Carpenter's last flight.

"Two-Upmanship"

Meanwhile, the Soviets were scrambling to manufacture more spacecraft. Both Glenn and Carpenter completed their missions without

Scott Carpenter was one of the few astronauts who flew only one space mission for NASA. Unaware of the flight director's resolve not to give him another mission, he spent time training underwater, using water's natural buoyancy to simulate the effects of weightlessness. He also helped NASA plan and build an underwater training facility for the astronauts.

In 1965, Carpenter took a temporary assignment as an aquanaut aboard *Sealab*, the Navy's underwater habitat. His research included living and working for 30 days on the ocean floor off La Jolla, California. Later, Carpenter also worked with the famous oceanographer Jacques Cousteau.

Now retired from NASA and the Navy, he runs the Scott Carpenter Man in the Sea Program, a school in Key Largo, Florida. The school trains people to work and live in the ocean and features an underwater hotel.

Carpenter has also written several books, including two adventure novels

Scott Carpenter just prior to liftoff aboard *Aurora 7*

that he calls "underwater techno-thrillers." *The Steel Albatross,* published in 1991, featured the adventures of a Navy hero on duty aboard a high-tech stealth submarine. A sequel, *Deep Flight,* came out in 1994.

any competing headlines from the Soviet Union. A year passed without any further crewed missions. Then, on August 11, 1962, *Vostok 3* was launched, followed the next day by *Vostok 4*, placed in a higher orbit. The Soviets had placed two crewed spacecraft in orbit at once. It was the first "tandem" spaceflight. The two Vostoks came within 3.2 miles (5 km)—close enough to catch sight of each other.

The world was impressed. "TWO-UPMANSHIP" was the headline carried by one London newspaper. Even in the United States, morale flagged. The prominent American physicist Edward Teller remarked, "There is no doubt that the best scientists as of this moment are not in the U.S., but in Moscow."

A closer look showed that the Vostok flights included no new technology. Newspaper reporters assumed that the Soviets had achieved advances in pilot control that would allow the "station keeping" and docking maneuvers required for building space stations or going to the Moon. However, that wasn't the case, and the Soviets never claimed it was. Still, NASA had nothing so glitzy waiting in the wings.

Instead, the next Mercury mission would be solid and as near to technical perfection as possible.

The Textbook Flight

That was the challenge shouldered by Wally Schirra on the Mercury 8 mission, aboard *Sigma 7*. Schirra was a crack pilot with a fine hand on the controls—a perfect choice.

On the morning of October 3, 1962, Schirra smiled at the car ignition key he found hanging in the capsule when he crawled through the hatch and settled onto the couch. The ground crew knew he would appreciate the tension breaker—Schirra was known for his sense of

Sigma 7, Wally Schirra's textbook flight, heads for space.

Wally Schirra is the only astronaut to fly in all three programs designed to land humans on the Moon—Mercury, Gemini, and Apollo. He logged 295 hours in space, more time than any of the other Mercury Seven. For Gemini, he commanded *Gemini 6A* with pilot Thomas Stafford. His spacecraft completed a successful *rendezvous* in space with *Gemini 7*, which was in orbit at the same time. He also served as commander of *Apollo 7*, the first crewed test of the newly designed Apollo equipment after the *Apollo 1* tragedy. He and his crewmates flew in Earth orbit for 260 hours—nearly 11 days—and the mission was a success. All three astronauts suffered from head colds, though, and became a bit grumpy.

Thinking that additional mission assignments were unlikely, Schirra resigned from NASA and the Navy in 1969. He once remarked, "I didn't want to be a potted palm." He directed several companies, formed his own consultant firm, Schirra

Enterprises, and later sold it and retired. He is also the author of several books, including *Schirra's Space* and *From Wildcats to Tomcats* (about naval aviation). Ever the flier, when asked whether he would want to return to space on the Space Shuttle, he replied, "Not unless I could fly it. I'm not interested in sitting in back."

Wally Schirra ready for liftoff aboard *Gemini 6A* in 1965

humor. Countdown proceeded fairly smoothly, and the big Atlas rocket thundered into the air. "I have liftoff," Schirra yelled to Deke Slayton through the microphone, "and she feels real nice."

Ten seconds later, as the big rocket lifted from the pad, it made hearts stop. It had begun to roll clockwise, and the condition was serious—just 20 percent more roll, and the mission would abort. Then, suddenly, the rolling stopped and the Atlas straightened out. Everyone breathed a sigh of relief. The problem turned out to be caused by misaligned steering engines, but the Atlas did its job. Schirra was lucky.

After that, the mission went incredibly smoothly. Even so, like Carpenter, Schirra found three times that he had accidentally turned on both the manual and automatic thruster controls at once. Having both systems running used up huge amounts of fuel unnecessarily and could have caused the same problems Carpenter had. Thanks to warnings from Carpenter and the debriefing that followed the Mercury 7 mission, Schirra was looking out for the problem, and caught the mistake right away.

Otherwise, Schirra put *Sigma 7* through its paces. All systems operated well, and everything was on schedule. He splashed down in the Pacific Ocean—the first Mercury mission to do so—only 5 miles (8 km) from the aircraft carrier. When Schirra arrived aboard the ship after splashdown, he proclaimed the mission a "textbook flight." When NASA completed its review, its engineers made the same judgment. According to the official NASA account of the mission, "The quality of the mission, of the hardware, of the software, of procedures, and of the pilot were all superb." In short, Wally Schirra's Mercury 8 mission was A-OK.

The "Day-Long" Mercury

Gordon Cooper was born and grew up in Shawnee, Oklahoma, and he had a strong Oklahoma twang. He was a hotshot flier and he had a reputation for irritating NASA bureaucrats by buzzing their offices with a low-flying jet. But he was a good astronaut.

His launch was next, and it would be a long one. Cooper's flight aboard *Faith 7* was billed as the "day-long mission," the longest stay in space yet for a U.S. astronaut. The Soviets dampened this success slightly 1 month later with a mission that lasted 81 orbits, compared to Cooper's 22.5 orbits. Still, Cooper's flight nearly quadrupled the longest Mercury flight to date.

During his 34 hours and 20 minutes in space, Cooper had his share of trouble. A light flashed to indicate that he was descending, but it was wrong. He couldn't check the spacecraft's attitude position, unless he looked out the window. Cooper's automatic control system failed, and he had to bring *Faith 7* in by manual control—without instruments. By the end of his flight, nearly every system had failed on him, but he splashed down safely in the Pacific Ocean, only 4 miles (6.4 km) from the recovery carrier—beating Wally Schirra's 5-mile (8-km) record.

After Cooper's flight, almost 2 years passed before the next piloted U.S. spacecraft took off. Cooper was the last astronaut ever to fly solo in space. The next mission would mark the beginning of Project Gemini—two astronauts in a spacecraft on each mission. Gemini was the next step toward the Moon.

After flying the final mission of Project Mercury, Gordon Cooper went on to command *Gemini 5*, the first U.S. long-endurance flight. In the process he and his crewmate, Pete Conrad, set a new international record of 8 days in space. The record held for 5 years. The exercise may have been boring, but the mission proved that astronauts could survive zero gravity for the length of time it would take to go to the Moon, land, and return.

In 1970, Cooper resigned from NASA and joined Walt Disney Productions as vice president of research and development. He later became president of the Galaxy Group, a small firm in Van Nuys, California, that restores, designs, and builds aircraft. Cooper also serves on the board of directors of the Give the Kids the World Foundation and the Astronaut Scholarship Foundation. He still flies whenever he can. When interviewed recently, Cooper remarked that he'd return to space in a second, if anyone offered him the chance, adding, "But what I'm really holding out for is a Mars mission."

Astronauts Gordon Cooper (right) and Eugene Cernan (left) aboard the Gemini spacecraft

Chapter 7

Beyond Mercury

O verall, Project Mercury was a success. It had achieved its goal of sending humans to space. It had also shown that, with training and preparation, astronauts could function extremely well in this strange and alien environment. It proved that engineers and scientists could solve the problems of building the rockets, spacecraft, spacesuits, and other equipment needed for survival in space.

There were also failures, such as automatic controls that didn't work, hatch bolts that blew off for no apparent reason, a missed landing site, and a rolling launcher. These were grim reminders of the risks that accompany every ride into space. Only random chance, or "luck," kept real disaster from plaguing the Mercury missions—not because of fault, or neglect, or poor design, but because the giant machines and

These Mercury astronauts—Alan Shepard (right), Gus Grissom (center), and John Glenn (left)—were the first three U.S. astronauts to venture into space.

One of the many Space Shuttle missions of the 1990s, this *Discovery* mission included Mercury pioneer U.S. Senator John Glenn as a payload specialist.

their interactions were so complex that some failures were inevitable. What was true then is still true today, and the risks of space travel continue to exist—but so do the benefits, the challenges, and the adventure.

Within 2 years, from 1962 to 1963, six U.S. astronauts had flown in space on Mercury spacecraft, and four of them had orbited Earth. The astronauts had shown they could control their spacecraft under the harsh conditions of space, and they had all survived. The Mercury Project had cost a little more than $400 million and employed more than 2 million people in the government and in the aerospace industry.

Mercury had made the first step toward the Moon. When Gordon Cooper's *Faith 7* splashed down, the Gemini and Apollo programs were already underway. NASA had 2,500 people working at the Manned Spacecraft Center in Houston, Texas, but by 1963, only 500 were still working on Mercury. The others were already working on future missions to the Moon.

Most important of all, the Mercury Project was the first toehold for climbing beyond the cradle of Earth's atmosphere into the vast regions of space. It was the beginning of many new and exciting possibilities. It was the beginning of a space program that now includes several Space Shuttle flights each year, the construction of a new *International Space Station*, exploration of the planets by dozens of robotic spacecraft, and a thousand satellites orbiting Earth. We have indeed come a long way since Alan Shepard's historic flight on May 5, 1961.

Vital Statistics

Spacecraft	Date of Launch	Astronauts	Highlights
MERCURY 2	January 31, 1961	Ham, a chimpanzee	First passenger on a suborbital Mercury flight, 16.5 minutes
FREEDOM 7	May 5, 1961	Alan Shepard	First American in space, suborbital flight, 15 minutes
LIBERTY BELL 7	July 21, 1961	Gus Grissom	Suborbital flight, 16 minutes
MERCURY 5	November 29, 1961	Enos, a chimpanzee	First passenger on an orbital Mercury flight; 2 orbits
FRIENDSHIP 7	February 20, 1962	John Glenn	First American orbital flight; 3-orbits, 4.9 hours
AURORA 7	May 24, 1962	Scott Carpenter	3 orbits, 4.9 hours
SIGMA 7	October 3, 1962	Wally Schirra	8 orbits, 9.25 hours
FAITH 7	May 15, 1963	Gordon Cooper	22.5 orbits, 34.3 hours

Project Mercury: A Timeline

1957 The former Soviet Union launches the first artificial satellite, *Sputnik 1*.

1958 The United States launches its first satellite, *Explorer 1*.

1961 The first test flight of a Mercury spacecraft and Atlas rocket carries Ham the chimpanzee into space and safely back to Earth.

The first piloted Mercury flight carries Alan Shepard into space aboard *Freedom 7*.

Gus Grissom becomes the second American in space aboard *Liberty Bell 7*.

The first orbital test flight with a passenger carries Enos the chimpanzee into space and safely back to Earth.

1962 — John Glenn becomes the first U.S. astronaut to orbit Earth aboard *Friendship 7*.

Scott Carpenter aboard *Aurora 7* completes a second U.S. orbital flight.

Wally Schirra extends time in space to more than 9 hours aboard *Sigma 7*.

1963 — In last Mercury flight, Gordon Cooper, aboard *Faith 7*, nearly quadruples the longest Mercury flight to date with 34.3 hours in space.

Glossary

attitude—the position of a spacecraft in flight in relation to a fixed reference such as the horizon or another vehicle; also, a spacecraft's orientation with respect to the direction it is moving

biosensor—one of a group of electrodes used to track heartbeat, breathing, and other important body functions

booster—an extra rocket (sometimes called a booster rocket) used to give an additional boost, or lift, to the main cargo and rocket. As a booster rocket uses up its fuel, it is discarded and falls back to Earth. Some empty booster rockets can be collected and reused.

centrifuge—a machine that spins to simulate the increased gravity of liftoff, reentry, and braking

extravehicular activity (EVA)—a space walk; activity outside a spacecraft

intercontinental ballistic missile (ICBM)—a rocket developed for military purposes, but sometimes used for launching spacecraft

jettison—to cast off or discard

multistage rocket—a rocket system that makes use of one or more booster rockets to provide additional lift

orbit—the path an object follows as it revolves around another object in space

payload—the amount of cargo carried by a spacecraft or rocket

pitch—movement causing the nose of a spacecraft to lift or descend in relation to the rear

rendezvous—to meet, to be in the same area at the same time; also, as a noun, a meeting or encounter

retrofire—to become ignited

satellite—an object that orbits another object. Natural satellites include planets, asteroids, or comets that orbit the Sun or a moon that orbits a planet or an asteroid. Many artificial satellites, such as the Sputnik and Gemini spacecraft, have been launched into space by humans.

suborbital—describes a launch that does not reach orbit, although it penetrates the region we call space

zero gravity—weightlessness

To Find Out More

The news from space changes fast, so it's always a good idea to check the copyright date on books, CD-ROMs, and video tapes to make sure that you are getting up-to-date information. One good place to look for current information from NASA is U.S. government depository libraries. There are several in each state.

Books

Burrows, William. *This New Ocean: A History of the First Space Age.* New York: Random House, 1998.

Campbell, Ann Jeanette. *The New York Public Library Amazing Space: A Book of Answers for Kids.* New York: John Wiley & Sons, 1997.

Cernan, Eugene, with Don Davis. *The Last Man on the Moon.* New York: St. Martin's Press, 1999.

Glenn, John, with Nick Taylor. *John Glenn: A Memoir.* New York: Bantam Books, Inc., 1999.

Grimwood, James M. *Project Mercury: A Chronology.* Washington, DC: NASA SP-4001, 1963.

Link, Mae Mills. *Space Medicine in Project Mercury.* Washington, DC: NASA SP-4003, 1965.

Schefter, James. *The Race: The Uncensored Story of How America Beat Russia to the Moon.* New York: Doubleday, 1999.

Schirra, Wally, with Richard N. Billings. *Schirra's Space*. Annapolis, MD: Naval Institute Press, 1995.

Slayton, Donald K., with Michael Cassutt. *Deke! U.S. Manned Space: From Mercury to the Shuttle*. New York: St. Martin's Press, 1994.

Spangenburg, Ray, and Diane Moser. *Space People from A to Z*. New York: Facts On File, Inc., 1990.

Swenson, Lloyd S., Jr., James M. Grimwood, and Charles C. Alexander. *This New Ocean: A History of Project Mercury*, republished edition. Washington, DC: NASA SP-4201, 1998.

Video Tapes

History of Spaceflight: Reaching for the Stars. Finley-Holiday Film Corp., 1995.

Mercury and Gemini Spacecraft Missions. Finley-Holiday Film Corp., 1988.

Organizations and Online Sites

Many of the sites listed below are NASA sites, with links to many other interesting sources of information about moons and planetary systems. You can also sign up to receive NASA news on many subjects via e-mail.

Astronomical Society of the Pacific
390 Ashton Avenue
San Francisco, CA 94112
http://www.aspsky.org/

The Astronomy Café
http://www2.ari.net/home/odenwald/cafe.html
NASA scientist Sten Odenwald answers questions and offers news and articles relating to astronomy and space.

Kennedy Space Center
http://www.ksc.nasa.gov/ksc.html
This site features an overview of shuttle flights as well as information about the Mercury, Gemini, and Apollo programs.

NASA Ask a Space Scientist
http://image.gsfc.nasa.gov/poetry/ask/askmag.html#list
NASA scientists answer your questions about, astronomy, space, and space missions. The site also has archives and fact sheets

NASA History
http://history.nasa.gov
This in-depth site has information about all aspects of NASA history.

NASA Human Spaceflight

http://spaceflight.nasa.gov/index-m.html

This is the Internet hub for exploring everything related to human spaceflight, including current stories and realtime data as they break. You can explore the *International Space Station,* track Space Shuttle flights, trace space history, and see plenty of interesting images.

NASA Newsroom

http://www.nasa.gov/newsinfo/newsroom.html

This site has NASA's latest press releases, status reports, and fact sheets. It includes a NASA News Archive for past reports and a search button for the NASA Web. You can even sign up for e-mail versions of all NASA press releases.

National Space Society

600 Pennsylvania Avenue, S.E., Suite 201
Washington, DC 20003
http://www.nss.org

The Planetary Society

65 North Catalina Avenue
Pasadena, CA 91106-2301
http://www.planetary.org

Places to Visit

Check the Internet (*www.skypub.com* is a good place to start), your local visitors' center, or phone directory for planetariums and science museums near you. Here are a few suggestions:

Exploratorium
3601 Lyon Street
San Francisco, CA 94123
http://www.exploratorium.edu
Internationally acclaimed interactive science exhibits, including astronomy subjects.

Jet Propulsion Laboratory (JPL)
4800 Oak Grove Drive
Pasadena, CA 91109
http://www.jpl.nasa.gov/faq/#tour
Tours available once or twice a week by arrangement; see web site for instructions, or write to the JPL visitor contact. JPL is the primary mission center for all NASA planetary missions.

Kansas Cosmosphere and Space Center
1100 N. Plum
Hutchinson, Kansas 67501
http://www.cosmo.org

Among other exhibits, this museum houses Robert Goddard's lab and the recovered Mercury capsule *Liberty Bell 7*, lifted from the ocean in July 1999. The museum oversaw the hunt for Grissom's lost spacecraft, paid for by the Discovery Channel. The capsule was delivered to the Cosmosphere, where it is bathed in a continuous spray of water. Restoration began immediately, in full view of public visitors.

Kennedy Space Center Visitor Center Complex
Kennedy Space Center, FL 32899
http://www.kennedyspacecenter.com
Sites and exhibits include the Rocket Garden, where rockets stand on display, an opportunity to meet an astronaut face to face, a historic tour of Mercury, Gemini, and Apollo launchpads, and two IMAX theaters.

NASA Goddard Space Flight Center
Code 130, Public Affairs Office
Greenbelt, MD 20771
http://pao.gsfc.nasa.gov/vc/info/info.htm
Visitors can see a Moon rock, brought back to Earth by Apollo astronauts, as well as other related exhibits.

Space Center Houston
Space Center Houston Information
1601 NASA Road 1
Houston, Texas 77058
http://www.spacecenter.org/

Offers a tour and exhibits related to humans in space, including the Apollo missions to the Moon.

U.S. Astronaut Hall of Fame

6225 Vectorspace Blvd.
Titusville, FL 32780
http://www.astronauts.org/
Opened in 1990, this center is dedicated to telling the stories of U.S. astronauts.

Index

Bold numbers indicate illustrations.

Ray Spangenburg and **Kit Moser** are a husband-and-wife writing team specializing in science and technology. They have written 38 books and more than 100 articles, including a five-book series on the history of science and a four-book series on the history of space exploration. As journalists, they covered NASA and related science activities for many years. They have flown on NASA's Kuiper Airborne Observatory, covered stories at the Deep Space Network in the Mojave Desert, and experienced zero-gravity on experimental NASA flights out of NASA Ames Research Center. They live in Carmichael, California, with their two dogs, Mencken (a Sharpei mix) and F. Scott Fitz (a Boston Terrier).